THE
SAMUEL MAY WILLIAMS
HOME

Library of Congress Cataloging-in-Publication Data

Henson, Margaret Swett, 1924–
  The Samuel May Williams Home: the life and neighborhood of an early
  Galveston entrpreneur / Margaret Swett Henson.
      p.   cm.   —(Fred Rider Cotten popular history series : no. 7)
  Includes bibliographical references.
  ISBN 0-87611-125-8 (pbk. : acid-free paper)
    1. Galveston (Tex.)—History. 2. Williams, Samuel May, 1795–1858. 3. Samuel
May Williams House (Tex.) 4. Bankers—Texas—Galveston—Biography.
5. Galveston (Tex.)—Buildings, structures, etc. I. Title. II Series.
F394.G2H46
976.4'139—dc20   92-28140
                                                                      CIP

©1992 by the Texas State Historical Association.
All rights reserved. Printed in the U.S.A.
Number seven in the Popular History Series
ISBN: 0-87611-125-8
Design by David Timmons

Published by the Texas State Historical Association in cooperation with the
Center for Studies in Texas History at the University of Texas at Austin.

Cover: The Samuel May Williams Home, 1988. Photograph by Jim Cruz. *Courtesy
Galveston Historical Foundation.*

THE
SAMUEL MAY WILLIAMS
HOME

The Life and Neighborhood
of an Early Galveston Entrepreneur

BY MARGARET SWETT HENSON

TEXAS STATE
HISTORICAL ASSOCIATION

CONTENTS

INTRODUCTION

THE SAMUEL MAY WILLIAMS HOUSE, the home of a founder of the Galveston City Company and Texas's first banker, is the second oldest house still standing on Galveston Island.* It was built in the winter of 1839–1840. Unlike so many historic homes, there is no eye-catching view of its front door because it sits sideways to the street. Moreover, modern homes and a few relics of the Victorian era line the street, leaving the visitor unaware of the once-grand view from the cupola when the house was isolated on twenty acres. Williams owned two ten-acre "outlots" that stretched from Avenue O on the north to Avenue Q on the south and from Thirty-fifth to Thirty-seventh streets.

From 1839 until the 1850s, Galveston's elite lived in comfortable suburban homes on the outlots south of Broadway and west of town. All were elevated on tall piers to be above the high storm tides that occasionally ravaged the island and also to catch the gulf breeze.

After Williams died in 1858, his heirs began disposing of the acreage, and by 1900 there were several homes along the well-defined Avenue P on the north side of the house. In recent years the street has been renamed Bernardo de Galvez for the Spanish governor who ordered a survey of the Texas coast in the 1780s and whose name was attached to the island by his mapmaker.

---

* The oldest house is that of Michel B. Menard on Thirty-third Street at Avenue N $^1/_2$, which is discussed later.

This house looks much as it did during Williams's lifetime except that the ten-foot brick piers on which it stood have been reduced to only three feet because of the grade-raising that occured after the devastating 1900 hurricane. The house survived the storm, but afterwards had about seven feet of sand pumped underneath, which obliterated the cisterns and buried most of the storeroom.

Philip C. Tucker, an administrator of Williams's estate, bought the house in 1859 and his descendants occupied it until 1953. Neglected for years, the old home faced destruction. Local preservationists incorporated the Galveston Historical Foundation in order to buy the historic site, the first of many landmarks saved by the organization.

At first it was opened to the public occasionally, but after lengthy study the GHF renovated the Williams house in the 1980s as a house museum open on a regular basis. The house was returned to its 1850s appearance including the rebuilding of the cupola, which had been destroyed by fire about 1890.

1.
A MAN "PROUD IN SPIRIT AND CHARACTER"

SAMUEL MAY WILLIAMS used that phrase describing himself in a letter to his wife in 1838, while he was in the United States on business for the new Republic of Texas.[1] He was a successful merchant and land speculator and a partner in the Galveston City Company, which had just held its first sale of lots in the island city. The new town attracted numerous immigrants from the United States who flocked to Texas after it had achieved its independence from Mexico in 1836.

Williams was born in Providence, Rhode Island, on October 4, 1795, the eldest son of a ship captain. In his early teens he joined his uncle's Baltimore commission house as an apprentice to learn bookkeeping and other aspects of international commerce. Sent as super-cargo to Buenos Aires at the close of the War of 1812, the young man remained in the cosmopolitan capital, where he mastered Spanish and French, for several years.[2]

By 1819 Williams was working in a New Orleans commission house, but in May 1822 he boarded a schooner for Mexican Texas, where his linguistic and clerical abilities were immediately useful. Williams was among the first Anglo Americans to leave the United States for Texas and a fresh start after the 1819 banking panic. The Mexican government offered both large grants of land and sanctuary for the unfortunate victims of foreclosures. Empresario Stephen F. Austin returned from Mexico City in 1823 with his colonization contract and employed Williams as his assistant, an arrangement that continued for more than a decade. In his elegant hand, Sam wrote all of the deeds in Spanish for the "Old Three Hundred," the name given those pioneers who filled Austin's first contract. During the empresario's many absences, the loyal lieutenant supervised Austin's land business for the subsequent four colonization contracts.[3]

Williams settled at San Felipe de Austin, the court town established by Austin on the Brazos River, where he married Sarah P. Scott in 1828. He was a busy bureaucrat, not only serving as Austin's right hand man, but also as collector of tonnage duties, dispenser of the stamped paper required for all legal documents, and secretary for the *ayuntamiento*, the town government whose reports to the state authorities had to be in Spanish. Because of a lack of circulating money on the Mexican frontier, Williams received remuneration in large land grants from the state for his duties. Beyond his headright of two leagues and three *labores* (9,387 acres), he received eleven leagues, bringing his holdings to over 58,000 acres. The canny businessman located portions along various waterways from the Colorado River to Buffalo Bayou, intending to sell to newcomers. Williams also speculated in land, as did the empresario himself. Poor men who could not pay the required fees to the state in order to receive their 4,428-acre headrights deeded one-half to those who could make the payments. Toward the end of the colonial period and the demise of the empresario system, conveniently located tracts could be sold to wealthy new Texans for fifty cents per acre.[4]

While land was the basis for Williams's wealth, he was a merchant at heart. In 1834, he became the junior partner in the firm of McKinney and Williams in their new town of Quintana at the mouth of the Brazos River. Williams and his partner complemented each other: Sam was the cautious bookkeeper, while Thomas F. McKinney was the gregarious contractor who bought Texas cotton and supervised transporting it to market. Six years younger than Sam, McKinney was an active outdoorsman, more interested in horse racing than in mercantile details. A native of Kentucky, McKinney had joined one of the first caravans from Missouri to Santa Fe in 1823 to trade manufactured goods for specie and livestock. His party found the Santa Fe market saturated and the residents without money, so McKinney continued south to

Chihuahua and then returned home through Coahuila to Texas. He received a headright on the Brazos River from Austin in 1824, but settled instead at Nacogdoches, where he had a store and traded with the Indians. In 1830 he moved his wife, Nancy, to San Felipe and went into business taking cotton to market in Coahuila by pack train and later to the Rio Grande by schooner until he joined Williams.[5]

In the 1830s commerce in Texas was hampered by the continued lack of circulating money, and in 1835 Sam Williams traveled to the state capital at Monclova (Texas was combined with its southern neighbor, Coahuila, because of low population) to ask for a bank charter allowing him to print small bills for use in Texas. The legislators approved the plan but before he could return home civil war threatened the state capital. President Antonio Lopez de Santa Anna personally led the army against the neighboring state of Zacatecas to punish it for opposing his new restrictive laws. The apprehensive representatives at Monclova feared that Coahuila-Texas would be his next target. In order to raise money and to recruit and equip volunteers to defend the state, the legislature awarded large tracts of vacant land on the Texas frontier to influential men. Sam Williams was one, and when Santa Anna suddenly returned to Mexico City, many Texans viewed the land grants as fraud, and labeled the participants as "speculators," a derogatory term at the time. The Consultation, a body of Anglo Texans provoked by Santa Anna's actions, met in November 1835, and among other acts declared the large grants null and void.[6]

When Santa Anna's army started towards the Brazos River at the end of March 1836, McKinney evacuated his wife and Sam's second wife Sarah Williams with her two boys, Austin and William, ages six and three, and her stepson, Joe, ten, the son of Sam's first marriage. Sarah carefully packed all of Sam's papers in a small trunk and took them on board the vessel that sailed to McKinney's warehouse near the mouth of the Neches River. Also on board were Mrs. William H. Jack, Mrs. James Walker Fannin, and their children all under the age of six. When the men left for the Texas army, their families stayed with McKinney. The pregnant Minerva Fort Fannin was already a widow, although she did not yet know about the massacre at Goliad.[7]

Samuel May Williams by unknown artist, ca. 1837. Oil on canvas, 25 x 19 ¹/₂ inches. *Courtesy Rosenberg Library, Galveston, Texas.*

Sarah Williams by unknown artist, ca. 1837. Oil on canvas, 25 x 19 ¹/₂ inches. The name "Leyin" is painted on the front of the portrait. *Courtesy Rosenberg Library, Galveston, Texas.*

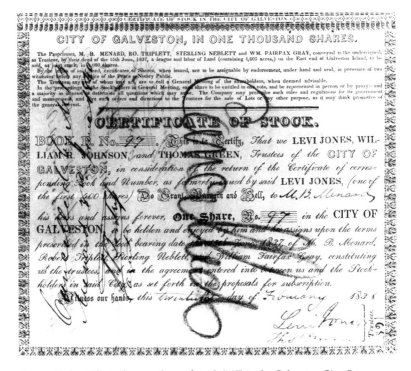

A cancelled certificate for one share of stock (#97) in the Galveston City Company dated 1838 and signed by Levi Jones. It was cancelled in 1840 by M. B. Menard and signed by Gail Borden, Jr., agent. *Courtesy Rosenberg Library, Galveston, Texas.*

When the Texans declared their independence from Mexico in March 1836, Williams was in the United States seeking funds to start his bank. Abandoning that project, he used his mercantile connections in New York, Philadelphia, and Baltimore to secure war supplies and ships to carry men and munitions to Texas. Meanwhile, McKinney took a similar course in Texas and New Orleans.[8]

The firm of McKinney and Williams contracted an indebtedness of over $99,000 supplying war materials to oppose Santa Anna, but the new Republic had no means to pay its many obligations. The leaders hoped to borrow money in the United States backed by the sale of vacant land. However, Texas's need for a loan coincided with the banking panic of 1837 and a severe constriction of credit;

thus Texas agents were unable to secure any money. The panic also ruined many of McKinney and Williams's creditors in the United States who expected immediate payment from the Texans, which would have endangered the firm. Nevertheless, the two men managed to stay afloat by diversifying their interests.[9]

Land on Galveston Island would be a partial solution to the firm's financial woes. Sam Williams and his partner had taken an early interest in Galveston Island at a time when Mexican policy forbade its occupation by foreigners. In 1833 McKinney's friend, Michel Branamour Menard, devised an ingenious scheme to acquire a foothold on the island by persuading a native Texan, Juan N. Seguin of San Antonio, to locate his bounty league and *labor* (4,605 acres for militia campaigns against the Indians) on the eastern end of the island. This ploy overcame the proscription against foreigners, and armed with a power of attorney from Seguin, Menard secured a survey and a title from the alcalde at Liberty in July 1834. To defray the costs of acquiring the best harbor on the Texas coast, Menard asked McKinney and Williams to take one-half interest which amounted to $200 each in what Menard called "the wild project of Galveston."[10]

Before the trio could utilize their title, friction between the Texans and Santa Anna erupted into revolution, which postponed economic development of the island. In December 1836, Menard applied to the first Texas Congress for confirmation of his Galveston title but other potential speculators objected. During the revolution,

A bank note for one dollar issued in 1848 by Samuel May Williams's Commercial & Agricultural Bank of Texas. *Courtesy Rosenberg Library, Galveston, Texas.*

capitalists in the United States had loaned money to the Texans in exchange for land certificates promising priority location rights. They and others with tenuous claims to the island jostled and maneuvered to acquire the Galveston harbor. To end the political wrangling and charges of favoritism, Congress demanded that Menard pay $50,000 within ninety days to secure his title. The Republic desperately needed money and this step seemed to solve its economic and political problems.[11]

The enterprising Menard had already increased the number of investors to include Augustus C. and John Kirby Allen, the New York brothers who had just established the new town of Houston, and Mosely Baker, who like J. K. Allen was a member of the First Congress. But to raise such a large sum quickly, Menard mortgaged his title to David White, a Mobile merchant; White immediately violated the agreement not to sell shares for less than face value and Menard had to buy back his interest. He managed to persuade a Kentucky capitalist, Robert Triplett, and his associates who had advanced money for the Texas revolution, to join in an expanded Galveston City Company. The new stock company issued one thousand $1,000 shares redeemable in city lots. The company employed John D. Groesbeck to survey and plat the town (to Fifty-sixth Street), and by early 1838 sales began among stockholders. At the first public sale in April, the investors and others bought home sites, business locations, and speculative tracts by paying one-fifth in cash as required by the charter. Menard, Williams, and McKinney were elected to the first board of directors along with Mosely Baker and John K. Allen.[12]

Even before the sale, McKinney had erected a three-story warehouse for the firm at the foot of Twenty-fourth Street across from the new customs house, and by July 1837 began building a wharf. But a hurricane struck the nascent town on October 6–7 and the high winds and water damaged the warehouse and pier and many of the vessels in the harbor. Williams was in the United States at the time, seeking a loan for the Republic and also contracting for naval vessels to defend Texas. McKinney made immediate repairs and with the financial backing of Henry Howell Williams, Sam's Baltimore brother (who had succeeded their uncle), the firm also built the Tremont Hotel, a tavern, a racetrack on the beach, and a number of rental houses.[13]

Thus Sam Williams and his partner were major developers of the new town supplying the necessary attractions for luring outside investors. The pair, with the aid of Henry Howell Williams, remained the leading commission house in the city until the mid-1840s. Williams and McKinney also took roles in local politics but lost out to more aggressive newcomers. While they were leading citizens, they led quiet social lives in keeping with their desires for privacy.

2.
THE HOUSE AND THE WILLIAMS FAMILY

SAM WILLIAMS RETURNED TO GALVESTON from the United States in June 1839 on board the schooner *San Jacinto*, one of the six war ships he had acquired for Texas. The citizens honored him with a public dinner and soon after elected him to represent them in the Fourth Congress of the Republic of Texas, the first to meet in the new capital at Austin.[1]

When Sam left for Austin in October 1839, he entrusted the building of his house to McKinney, who planned an identical structure for himself southwest of the Williams site. Nancy McKinney had moved from Quintana to one of the company-built houses in Galveston in mid-1838, but while Sam was in the United States Sarah stayed with her widowed mother on the lower San Jacinto River to await the birth of a fourth child. Mary Dorothea (Molly) was born in November 1838, before Sam returned. Sarah and the children briefly came to the island by steamboat when Sam came home, but returned to the comfort of her mother's home when he left to take his seat in Congress.[2]

In 1838 Williams had bought outlots 61 and 86 on either side of Avenue P between Thirty-fifth and Thirty-seventh streets. The land was valued for taxes at $5,000 in the inflated Texas currency. McKinney acquired lots 108 and 109 to the southwest between Avenues Q and R and straddling Forty-first Street. McKinney chose the more remote location because it skirted a bayou that carried his name and provided water for his livestock, and also because the firm's one and one-half mile race track circled twelve outlots between his home and the Gulf.[3]

Williams and his partner were not the first to build on the outlots; Menard had started a "fine" home north of the Williams site along the high ridge leading from town one year earlier. Suburban living was the choice of those who could afford the large lots. Not only was it quieter, it was healthier. Not understanding that mosquitos carried yellow fever, residents along the Gulf Coast blamed the seasonal epidemics on the fetid vapors rising from standing water, garbage, and cesspools in town. Outlot residents hoped that the splendid prevailing breeze off the Gulf would ensure the health of their families. Dr. Ashbel Smith, a Paris-trained surgeon, studied Galveston yellow fever patients in 1839 and noted that most cases occurred near the wharves and along the Strand. He concluded that the disease was not contagious, but came from "the decomposition of *abundant* animal and vegetable matters . . . and the exhalations from the extensive adjacent marsh. . . ."[4]

On December 10, 1839, McKinney wrote to Williams in Austin that the house was "under way." Local lore says that the Williams house was framed with white pine in Maine and shipped prefabricated to Galveston; this is partly correct. Ships from the northeast began coming fairly regularly to Galveston, bringing lumber cut in standard lengths and taking away Texas cotton. These same vessels brought a number of carpenters from Maine in 1838, due no doubt to the hard times in the United States. Preservation architects find no evidence that the house was prefabricated but confirm the use of northern white and yellow pine cut by a gang saw. The heavy timber sills supporting floor joists were assembled on the site with mortice and tenon joints and pinned with wooden dowels. This method was used also for the corner posts, sills, and plates.[5]

Williams and McKinney had doubtless agreed on the general style of the one and one-half story house based on tastes shaped by the popular Southern "raised cottage," prevalent along waterways from Louisiana to Alabama. The house, Classic Revival in style, faced east with a wide gallery stretching across both front and back. The south gallery was added a few years later. The wooden columns separated by wooden railings were in the Tuscan order and supported the wide overhanging roof that shaded the porches. Lapped, white-painted weatherboard siding sheathed the house.[6]

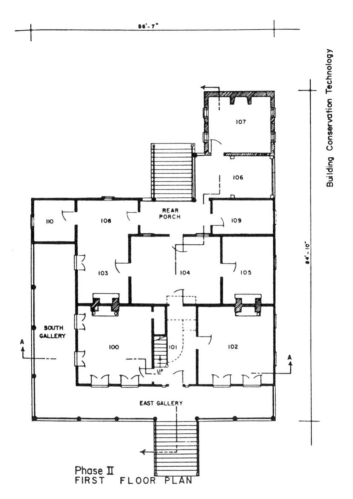

Floor plans (pages 14 and 15) and elevations (pages 16 and 17) of the Samuel May Williams house drawn by Building Conservation Technology in 1978 in preparation for restoration. They reflect the house as it stands today, restored to its condition in the years 1842–1860, including modifications made by Williams. *Courtesy Galveston Historical Foundation.*

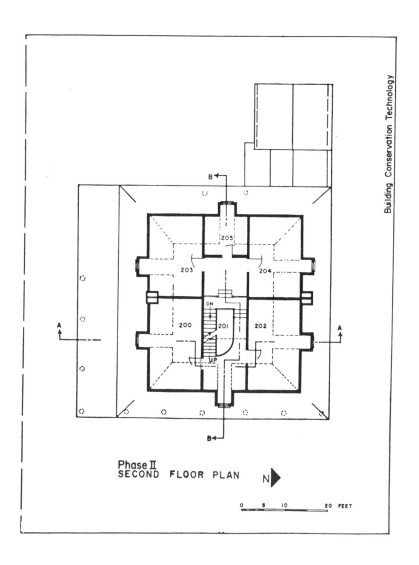

Phase Ⅱ
SECOND FLOOR PLAN   N ▶

0   5   10   20 FEET

15

Phase II East Elevation

Building Conservation Technology

The wood-shingled hipped roof with a flat deck boasted an enclosed cupola, a unique feature among the houses on the outlots. Single double-hung dormer windows ventilated the upper floor while standard sized double-hung windows with six-over-six lights served the first floor except on the front gallery. The four openings on the front porch facing east were French doors with panels below and eight glass lights above. Full-length dark gray louvered shutters protected all of the windows and allowed air to circulate even during rain storms. The front and back doors were centered and allowed a direct flow of air when opened.

The house rested on ten-foot-high brick piers. The hurricane in 1837 and living near the beach at Quintana convinced McKinney to build well above the storm tides. The ground floor was enclosed by wooden latticework and provided a place for a brick cistern to catch and store rain water and ample space to hang laundry in bad weather. A steep flight of thirteen steps from the ground to both the front and back galleries had simple wooden banisters and solid newel posts. A two-story detached brick building with the kitchen above and a storeroom below was on the northwest corner, and an

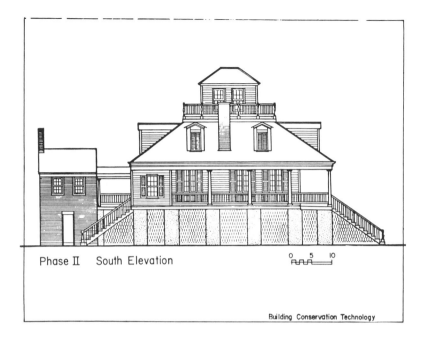

Phase II   South Elevation

0   5   10

Building Conservation Technology

elevated covered walkway connected the kitchen with the back gallery. A visitor noted in 1840 that a "white wooden fence" enclosed the "neat white" Williams house.[7]

Two brick interior chimneys served the four fireplaces on the first floor. The kitchen chimney was on its west wall, which consisted of a huge fireplace and a built-in oven.

The Williams owned only a few slaves—perhaps a family— for household servants and handymen. Their quarters were west of the house, along with a small stable and carriage house, plus a cowpen for the milk cow and a henhouse for the chickens. The family kept only enough animals to provide milk, cheese, butter, and eggs. A single-room schoolhouse may have been built near the house in 1842 to serve the neighborhood children. North of the house on the vacant outlot was a pasture, a cornfield for both the table and the animals, and a fenced vegetable garden. Like other women of her day, Sarah took pride in her vegetable garden, which might include peas, beans, eggplant, squash, cucumbers, melons, lettuce and even asparagus.[8]

Behind the front door, a wide hall with a staircase to the upper

17

floor divided two front rooms. One was Sam and Sarah's bedroom and the other a parlor, each having its own fireplace. The hall led into the commodious dining room that stretched across the back of the house sharing the width with a small bedroom on the north side used for guests or ill persons. The two fireplaces in the back rooms connected to the chimneys of the two front rooms. Upstairs were four bedrooms under the sloping roof, each with its dormer window, while the upstairs hall had dormers on the east and west. A unique feature is the stair landing which branches near the second floor, with three steps to the front and back.[9] The stair to the cupola rose above the main stair, and from the windows in the cupola one could see both the Gulf and the bay.

Although there are no photographs documenting the interiors, Williams's statements from merchants and his probate inventory give a fairly clear picture of the furnishings. Williams ordered the latest style in furniture, drapery, floor coverings, and accessories from Baltimore and New Orleans, adding new items from time to time. The house was well-furnished, not as elegant perhaps as homes in New Orleans, but as comfortable as any in Texas in the 1840s and 1850s.

The parlor had a fine piano, a sofa, chairs, a center table, and a book etagere. By 1851 Williams had installed stoves in the fireplaces for heating. Lighting, too, was up-to-date; in 1847 he bought a solar lamp, and similar lamps followed. Fashionable drapes hung at the windows and rugs or straw matting covered the floor depending on the season. The parents' bedroom had the usual fourposter bed with suitable hangings and covers for winter and summer, plus a marble-topped washstand, bureau, and armoire. Descriptions of the dining room are the least complete, but from the amount of ceramics, glass, and silver that the Williamses acquired, there must have been a sideboard and a table that could be expanded as needed. Only the piano and a siesta chair, a nineteenth century version of a lounge chair, have survived and are on exhibit in the house along with a few pieces of silver and knickknacks. Today's furnishings are representative of the era and match the inventories and statements as much as possible.[10]

In general this was a happy, family-oriented household. In 1842 a second daughter was born, Caroline Lucy (Caddy), and three years later the last child appeared, Samuel May, Jr. Sarah Williams suffered from cataracts, and in 1842 and 1844 traveled to Lexington, Kentucky, each time escorted by a son, to see a surgeon. Neither visit provided a cure and in 1854 she went to Boston, where a successful operation partially restored her sight.[11]

Williams gave his children the best education available. Joe and Austin went to school in Mobile under the care of their uncle, Nathaniel F. Williams, and later Austin and William attended Western Military Institute in Lexington. William went on to Harvard Law School. In 1852 Molly and Caddy enrolled in the Ursuline Academy on Avenue N and Twenty-fifth Street, where they could have music lessons and learn other lady-like accomplishments in addition to suitable academic subjects. At an early date the Williamses subscribed to *Godey's Ladies Book*, one of the major influences in determining feminine tastes in clothing, home decorating, literature, and music.[12]

One frightening experience took place in 1842 when the cook tried to poison the family while Sam was absent. Fortunately for Sarah her younger sister was visiting. Mary Jane Scott was able to seek help in restraining the slave who, according to legend, was locked in the storeroom to await Williams's return. Family papers fail to reveal what punishment awaited the malefactress, but such an offense usually resulted in a whipping or being sold to somebody at a distance who had not heard about the trouble.[13]

Tragedy struck in 1855, when little Sam died at age ten after a brief illness. His was the first death in the family and the first funeral to take place in the front parlor. Two years later Joe died in Trinity County and was buried there. After he lost his forearm while serving in the Mexican War, the young man tried to become a merchant. He began drinking heavily, however, and died at age thirty.[14]

While the family's life-style was not ostentatious, the Williamses lived comfortably although quietly. Entertainment was among family and close friends, perhaps in part because of Sarah's poor eyesight and seemingly shy nature. Three of the four surviving children married into well-known Galveston families, the Leagues and the Campbells, and remained in the neighborhood, while the other preferred living on the mainland. William H. Williams served as Galveston County Judge from 1874 through 1880. It was Sam's older daughter, Mary Dorthea League, the wife of Thomas Jefferson League, who preserved her father's papers through the 1900 hurricane; her son presented the large collection to the Rosenberg Library in 1923.

3.
1841–1858

*From Merchant to Banker
and the Death of a Founding Father*

"WE REGARD ALL BANKS AS EVIL"—
Houston *Telegraph and Texas Register,* January 10, 1848

THE ECONOMIC HARD TIMES following the Panic of 1837 continued into the early 1840s. The flow of gold and silver to international bankers forced Texas merchants to accept suspect paper notes, personal IOUs, and the greatly depreciated notes of the Republic of Texas, which sometimes sank to ten cents on the dollar.

To alleviate the shortage of coins in the Republic in 1841, Sam Williams successfully petitioned the Texas Congress for the privilege of issuing small-denomination paper money through the firm. The "Little Bank" circulated 25 and 50 cent notes, and one, two, and three dollar bills redeemable at par. That same year, the firm, the hotel, and even the race track had to be mortgaged to Henry Howell Williams of Baltimore to cover long-standing indebtedness, and Williams's brother sent his son to supervise the Galveston commission house. McKinney, a true Jacksonian, did not like banking and sold his interest in the firm in order to concentrate on his land holdings in Travis County and elsewhere. In 1850, the McKinneys moved permanently to their horse ranch on Onion Creek south of Austin, now preserved as McKinney Falls State Park.[1]

When Texas was annexed to the United States in 1845, Williams ran for a seat in the U.S. Congress but failed to win a majority of votes except in Galveston. He submerged his disappointment in work and in 1847 planned to activate the 1835 banking charter secured in Monclova and approved by the Texas Congress in 1836. The Commercial and Agricultural Bank, which could print and circulate its own money, opened on the corner of Twenty-third and Post Office streets in 1848; it was the first real bank in Texas. The bank's board of directors included Michel B. Menard and new Galveston merchants George H. Ball, Jacob L. Briggs, Henry Hubbell, and Benjamin A. Shepherd. Even though Williams had the required $100,000 in gold in his vault and similar credits in New Orleans and New York, in order to redeem his bank notes at par on demand, banking enemies determined to kill the bank.[2]

At this time, another newcomer, Robert Mills, formerly a commission merchant at Brazoria, opened a bank through his Galveston office. Instead of printing money, he circulated paper money from a defunct Mississippi bank after personally endorsing each bill. Even though Mills was careful not to call his enterprise a bank, the anti-banking faction targeted both men. Two months after the C&A Bank opened its doors, the Texas legislature passed a law against issuing paper money punishable by a $5,000 fine for each bill passed. In June 1848, the attorney general filed suit in the Galveston district court against Williams and eventually did the same against Mills. Over the next decade, while the hearings and appeals continued through the courts, Williams and Mills redeemed paper notes on demand and were model bankers. Finally, in February 1859, the Texas Supreme Court dismissed the Mills case but declared the C&A Bank unconstitutional—five months after the death of Sam Williams. The goodwill of the institution passed to Ball, Hutchings and Company, a commission house owned by former C&A Bank directors. Through this connection, the First Hutchings Sealy National Bank of Galveston, now part of NationsBank, can trace its roots to Sam Williams's bank.[3]

Williams's political beliefs during these years are unclear. When he ran for Congress in 1846, he said he was a "Jeffersonian democrat" in order to capitalize on the popularity of the national Democratic party, which had successfully annexed Texas to the United States. His Baltimore brother, however, was active in the Whig Party, as were many merchants and bankers. Williams's enemies called him a Whig and he perhaps could be counted among Galveston Whigs voting in the presidential elections in 1848 and

1852.[4] His attitude towards the growing crisis about extending slavery into the territories is unknown. He seemed more interested in banking than politics towards the end of his life.

Sam Williams died on September 13, 1858, at age sixty-three after a brief illness. Williams was a long-time Mason and the black-plumed Knights Templar conducted a ceremony at the house and served as pallbearers to escort the founder of their chapter to the Episcopal cemetery. An impressive cortege of Masonic groups, ship captains, city and state dignitaries, and friends followed the coffin as it passed the large crowd lining the dusty streets.[5]

Williams died without a will and the court named his lawyer-son William and fellow Mason Philip C. Tucker to settle the tangled estate. Williams left property valued at $95,000 plus large tracts of land in litigation. Before matters were settled, Sarah Williams also died. The four surviving children divided the property and sold the ten-acre homesite to Tucker.[6] Mary Dorothea League and William H. Williams built homes on the northern ten-acre tract.

From 1859 until 1954, the old Williams residence belonged to the Tucker family. Philip Tucker was born in Vermont in 1826. He became a lawyer and arrived in Texas in 1852. His first wife died childless, and in 1863 he married Mary Cecelia Labadie, the daughter of Dr. Nicholas D. Labadie, who bore him five children. When she died ten years later at age thirty-five, he married again, then once more, and his fourth wife, Isabella T. Baldwin, bore him two more children in the 1880s. Tucker was very active in the Freemasons and held various offices at local and state levels. In 1893 he was named to a national post in the Masonic order, and the family moved to Washington, D.C. He died in the nation's capital the following year and his widow and children returned to the old home in Galveston. It was at this time that the ten-acre homesite was divided among the Tucker heirs, with the widow and Tucker's oldest daughter Mary Cecelia, then twenty-eight, inheriting the house and the yard as it now exists.[7]

Before the family moved to Washington a fire in the upstairs rooms had destroyed the roof and cupola, and the latter was not rebuilt. Mary Cecelia never married and outlived her stepmother. She died in 1953 and her estate was handled by a bank which sold the historic home to the newly incorporated Galveston Historical Foundation.[8]

This photograph (6 ³/₈ x 4 ¹/₄ inches) of an unknown painting of Samuel May Williams in his Knights Templar uniform was made by Henry Morris in Galveston. *Courtesy Rosenberg Library, Galveston, Texas.*

Saving the Williams-Tucker house increased Galveston's awareness of its unique collection of Victorian architecture. Soon the Galveston Historical Foundation became the leader in preserving the island's architectural heritage. Restoring the Williams house to its 1850s appearance was challenging, but the result allows visitors to see how a well-to-do family lived on Galveston Island before mid-century.

If Sam Williams were to return today, he might be confused by his old neighborhood but he would recognize the home in which he lived for eighteen years.

4.
SAM WILLIAMS'S NEIGHBORHOOD

IN 1840 A USUALLY CYNICAL BRITISH VISITOR praised the island's leaders as men of "talent, worth & respectability." Francis C. Sheridan found some of the local customs strange, however. He met McKinney on board a steamer from Velasco to Galveston and was intrigued by his frock coat, made from scarlet blanket material edged in black, and was astounded to find another man in an identical coat of green. Sheridan called the firm of McKinney and Williams the "Barings (a major British banking house) of Texas," but was appalled when McKinney used his Bowie knife to pick his teeth.[1] Knowing what a European expected of Texans, McKinney obligingly provided colorful copy for Sheridan's book!

Seven of the business elite, land speculators and merchants, built homes near Williams, as shown on the 1845 William H. Sandusky map. Some, like McKinney, Menard, and the Bordens, were old friends of the Williamses while the others—John H. Sydnor, Samuel Slater, and James Love—scattered on outlots south of Broadway and west of Twenty-fifth Street were newcomers to Texas. In 1839 the Galveston City Company employed Sandusky to remap the city with slight adjustments to Groesbeck's plat of the previous year.[2] The exact date of his placing the tiny houses on the map cannot be determined, and Galveston deed records fail to be helpful because not all lots were recorded immediately. It is important to note that until May 1838 Galveston Island was part of Harris County, while the mainland belonged to Brazoria County. Thus the first deeds to property on the island were recorded in Harris County and later re-recorded in Galveston.

McKinney's home on the southwest corner of Avenue Q and Forty-first Street was completed in early 1840. But Mac and his wife were separated by that time and were divorced in 1842 on charges of mutual abandonment. Couples dissolving their marriages had to apply first to Congress and then have a hearing in the district court. Nancy was childless, which may have been part of their disagreement, and perhaps Mac, at age thirty-nine, had already become enamored of a new resident of Galveston, twenty-one-year-old Anna Gibbs. In September 1840, he sold the house and its adjacent lot on the east to Anna and the rest to her sister. Their mother, Mrs. Ellen M. Gibbs, a widowed Massachusetts school teacher, had moved to the island from Alabama in November 1838 at the urging of Sam Williams's brother in Mobile. The mother signed notes for very modest sums payable in two and three years. Anna and Mac married soon after his divorce. Although some of the neighbors continued to correspond with Nancy McKinney, who moved to Velasco, Anna was accepted by Galveston society. Anna loved horses as much as her doting husband and rode daily on the beach, but like her predecessor Anna bore no children. McKinney became the guardian of Pinckney and Minerva Fannin after their mother's death in 1839, and the girls lived with the McKinneys after 1842.[3]

West of the Williams residence was that of Thomas H. Borden, who erected a windmill on his property to pump water. Shallow wells on the island proved to be brackish and most residents depended on cisterns to catch rain water. Some early residents placed barrels in the sand dunes to collect rain water, and for a while, carts brought water from the freshwater lakes six miles west of town. A native of New York, Borden was the first of his family to leave his father's home in Indiana for Austin's colony in 1824. Besides farming, he made surveys for the empresario. In 1835 he joined his brother, Gail, Jr., in publishing the *Telegraph and Texas Register* in San Felipe and later Houston. He had married Demis Woodward in 1829, and after her death seven years later he moved to Galveston and married again. In 1849 the Thomas Borden family left the island for New Orleans.[4]

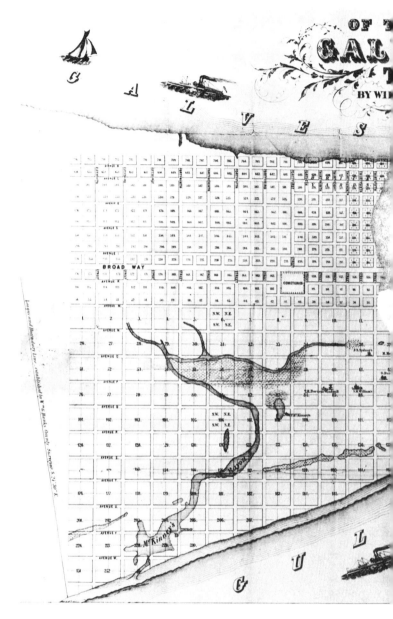

Plan of the City of Galveston, Texas by William H. Sandusky, 1845. Lithograph 27 ¹/₂ x 37 ¹/₂ inches. *Courtesy Rosenberg Library, Galveston, Texas.*

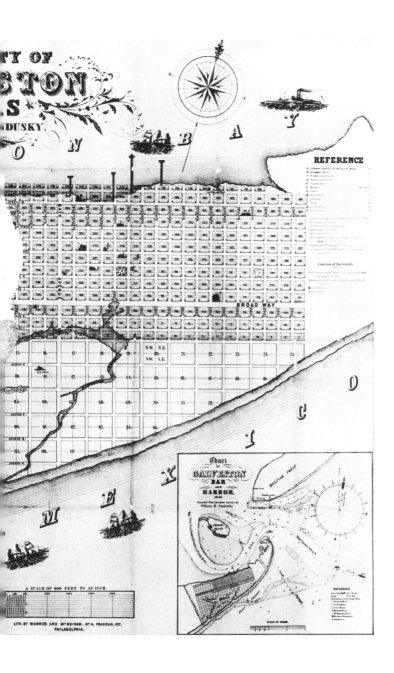

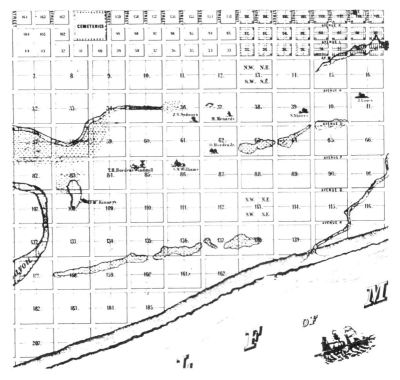

Details of Sandusky's plan showing (above) the outlots between Broadway and the Gulf of Mexico where Williams and others located their homes, and (right) the commercial wharf area on Galveston Bay. *Courtesy Rosenberg Library, Galveston, Texas.*

Gail Borden, Jr., a man of many talents, built his home northeast of the Williams house on Avenue O and Thirty-fifth Street. Born in 1801, Gail left Indiana for health reasons and married Penelope Mercer in Mississippi in 1829. They came to Texas the next year. Gail surveyed land for Austin and also was an assistant to Sam Williams in the San Felipe land office. When Santa Anna advanced towards the Brazos in 1836, Gail moved the land records and the printing press to Harrisburg where the new Texas government located temporarily. The press was destroyed when Santa Anna burned Harrisburg, but the Bordens bought new machinery in mid-1836 and continued their newspaper in Columbia and then Houston. President Sam Houston named Gail collector of customs at

Galveston in 1837, but he lost his position when Mirabeau Buonaparte Lamar became the second president of Texas in 1838. When Houston returned to the presidency in 1841, he reappointed Gail to the customs house. In the interim Gail became secretary and agent for the Galveston City Company, a position he held until he left the island. Penelope Borden died in 1844, leaving seven children, and the following year Gail married Augusta F. Sterne, a widow from Massachusetts. His inventive and eccentric mind produced a wagon equipped with a sail for use along the beach and in the water and also a wheeled dressing room so that modest ladies could ride into the Gulf and emerge in the water. His more significant inventions were a canned meat biscuit and, after leaving Galveston, condensed milk. The effort to secure a patent for the meat biscuit caused him to move to New York City in 1851.[5]

Menard's house on outlot 37 on Thirty-third Street was north of Gail Borden's home. The chain of title to this property is incomplete. In 1839 A. C. Allen listed outlot 37 among the property owned in partnership with his brother, who had died in August 1838. For this reason some researchers concluded that Allen had

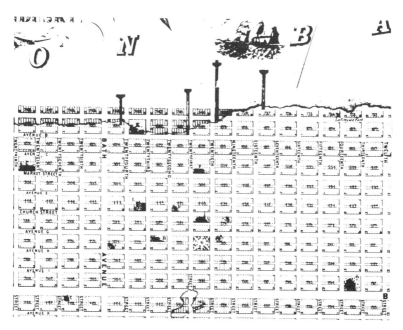

Thomas F. McKinney by unknown photographer, ca. 1850. Daguerreotype, 3 x 2 ¹/₂
inches. *Courtesy Texas State Library.*

Gail Borden and son, ca. 1840s. Daguerreotype, 3 x 2 ¹/₂ inches. *Courtesy Rosenberg Library, Galveston, Texas.*

Michel B. Menard. Photograph of an unknown painting, 6 ³/₄ x 4 ³/₄ inches. *Courtesy Rosenberg Library, Galveston, Texas.*

built the house.[6] This assumption is open to question, given the known activities of Menard and Allen between 1838 and 1843 partially explained below.

Poorly educated but shrewd, Michel Branamour Menard was one of Galveston's most colorful characters. He was born near Montreal in 1805 and entered John Jacob Astor's fur trading company at age fourteen. About 1823 he joined his well-to-do uncle, Pierre Menard, merchant and former territorial lieutenant governor of Illinois, at Kaskaskia, where he learned polite manners and some English. He became a trader to a band of Shawnee for his uncle's trading house, Menard and Valle, and moved with the tribe to northeastern Arkansas and then to the Red River above Natchitoches. By 1829 Menard visited Nacogdoches and met McKinney. Michel continued to buy pelts from Texas Indians to send to Menard and Valle to repay his indebtedness and also began speculating in Texas land in 1833. He bought unlocated large grants made to native Mexicans and recorded the claims in strategic places. With his cousin, Peter J. Menard, he built a sawmill and grist mill on one of these tracts along the lower Trinity River just above the town of Liberty. He was living there when he developed the Galveston scheme.[7]

Menard's personal life was a series of tragedies. His bride, Dianne LeClere of St. Louis, died of cholera en route to Texas in 1833. In 1837 he married a cousin, Catherine Maxwell of Kaskaskia, and began building her a "fine" house on the island. But she died of childbed fever the following summer.[8] The bereaved man seems to have sold the property to A. C. and J. K. Allen, perhaps to clear a debt.

By the time Menard married a third time in 1843, he had regained the home through purchases made by his cousin Peter, who deeded the tract to the new Mrs. Menard. Like McKinney deeding his property to Anna, this step protected it from creditors during the hard times. Mrs. Mary Jane (Clemens) Riddle Menard, formerly of St. Louis, lived in the house only four years before her death at age thirty-three in December 1847. Within two years Michel took a fourth wife, widow Rebecca Mary Bass, a native of Georgia who had two daughters whom Michel adopted. In early 1850 she bore Michel his only son, Doswell, who was named for Menard's

GALVESTON, FROM THE GULF SHORE

This lithograph by Charles Hooten (3 ³/₈ x 5 ¹/₈ inches) shows Galveston as viewed from the Gulf of Mexico. It appeared in Hooten's book *St. Louis' Isle, or Texiana,* published in London in 1847. *Courtesy Rosenberg Library, Galveston, Texas.*

Galveston business associate, J. Temple Doswell. It was probably at this time that Menard added wings to the basic structure making it into a show place that was the scene of the first Mardi Gras ball in Galveston. Menard died at his home in 1856 at age fifty-one from a cancer on his back. His widow remarried, but her son, Doswell Menard, inherited the house. In 1880 the house was sold to Edwin Ketchum, whose heirs held the property for a number of years before disposing of the old house.[9] In June 1992 the Galveston Historical Foundation, aided by the National Trust for Historic Preservation, bought the landmark.

The map shows the house of John S. Sydnor west of the Menard property on the corner of Avenue O and Thirty-fifth Street. A Virginia native, Sydnor visited Texas in 1838 and brought his family to Galveston two years later along with material for a house. The continuing hard times led the hard-working merchant to develop a large vegetable garden and dairy to help stock his store. To ease the shortage of coins, he issued tickets as change that circulated as money in town. Like other merchants Sydnor had difficulty in collecting debts owed to him, and often accepted livestock, land, and slaves to cancel overdue accounts on his books. There is no evidence that he regularly sold slaves as some have charged, but like other merchants, the auctioneer had to dispose of the blacks acquired in the payment of debts. He moved away from his suburban home about 1845, when he built a brick wharf and a warehouse at the foot of Twentieth Street and the Powhattan House, a hotel on Twenty-first Street between Avenues M and N. Sydnor served as Galveston's mayor in 1846–1847 and continued his business until 1868 but died the following year.[10]

East of the Menard House on Twenty-ninth Street, just north of some freshwater ponds, was Samuel Slater's residence. Little is known about the Massachusetts native, but fellow New Englander

THE "FEVER" BURIAL GROUND.
See Page 44.

Hullmandel & Walton Lithographers

The "Fever" Burial Ground, a Charles Hooten lithograph (3 ³/8 x 4 ⁷/8 inches), was published in his 1847 book *St. Louis' Isle, or Texiana. Courtesy Rosenberg Library, Galveston, Texas.*

Lucy Shaw told her mother in 1840 that he was "one of the best men we have from Boston," and praised the fine melons he grew on his place. Slater had come to Texas in 1839 and settled on the island where he paid taxes through 1847. He kept a few cows and horses and bought three blacks to help on his farm.[11]

The most eastern of the occupied outlots depicted on Sandusky's map is that of James Love near Avenue N and Twenty-ninth Street. Born in Kentucky in 1795, Love studied law and served in the Kentucky Assembly from 1818 to 1820 and in the Legislature a decade later; in 1833 he was elected to the United States Congress. He visited Houston in 1837 and brought his wife, Lucy Ballinger, and their two children to Galveston in 1839. An outspoken member of the Whig Party in the United States, he aligned himself in Texas with the Lamar faction opposing Sam Houston. He was a close friend of Gen. Albert Sidney Johnston and they invested in a cotton plantation on the Brazos River in the 1840s. Love became a merchant and a land speculator, especially in Galveston lots, and was a director of the City Company. He was a delegate to the Convention in 1845 that approved joining the United States and adopted a state constitution. The following year Love was appointed judge of the First Judicial District but resigned in 1849 to become clerk of the United States District Court in Galveston. In the 1850 census he reported property worth $40,000, and was the fifth-wealthiest man in Galveston following Gail Borden, Menard, newcomer James K. Brown, and the firm of Doswell & Hill, in which Menard was a silent partner.[12]

While men dominated business, politics, and even family matters in the first half of the nineteenth century, women on Galveston Island had feminine pursuits beyond the usual devotion to the care of their families. Without the convenience of telephones, women visited each other regularly to exchange news and gossip. Informal parties focused on the enjoyment of seasonal produce—watermelons, cantaloupes, figs, and dewberries. Sea bathing was also popular. As early as 1835, Mary Austin Holley watched some women enjoying the surf near the mouth of the Brazos River and the summer pastime continued a decade later at Galveston Island.[13]

In 1846 Martha Hopkins Barbour, granddaughter of Congressman Samuel Hopkins of Kentucky, made a long visit at the Galveston

This photograph appeared in the 1873 Galveston City Directory with the caption, "An Old Plantation House." *Courtesy Rosenberg Library, Galveston, Texas.*

home of her aunt Lucy V. Jones, the wife of Dr. Levi Jones, a director of the Galveston City Company. Martha's husband, Maj. Phillip N. Barbour, left her on the island when he departed for the Rio Grande with Albert Sidney Johnston to participate in the Mexican War. Martha and her cousins visited the McKinney home where "It is always pleasant . . . Mr. and Mrs. McKinney are so kind." Anna even allowed Martha to ride Randle, her "celebrated riding horse," along the beach, and occasionally Martha and Sally Jones spent the night, playing the piano with "Pink" and Minerva Fannin. During the summer, they went bathing in the Gulf under the guidance of Eliza Johnston, the general's young wife. Although Martha's husband had forbidden going into the Gulf, Martha was "induced" to try a sea bath which "felt so good . . . if I took one each day I would be robust" because it gave her an appetite. After the waves knocked her down, she went into town and bought an oil cap at Doswell's store and soon bragged that she could float while resting on her hands and thought that perhaps she might learn to swim.[14]

Not only did some adults and older children venture into the Gulf, but Sam Williams sent the servants to bring water in barrels to bathe little Mary and Caddy, who were suffering from the heat. Evidently the unpalatable but drinkable cistern water was hoarded during dry spells.[15]

The use of the Gulf shows that Galvestonians learned to adapt to the island's semi-tropical summers, although proper gentlemen continued to wear their coats in the presence of ladies. Before the Civil War the islanders were more cosmopolitan than some inland communities and followed the summer life-style of the East Coast's resorts.

The suburban outlots became less popular in the 1850s when the new elite began building fashionable homes along Broadway and in the east end of the city. Also, the pioneer leaders—Menard, McKinney, Williams, and the Bordens—moved away or died during the decade and the large lots were subdivided. Nevertheless, some families continued to build homes along Avenues O and P, although not many occupied entire ten-acre tracts as had the early residents. By 1850 Galveston was the largest town in Texas, with a population of 4,177. It would double in size in a decade and triple in two, retaining its preeminence in Texas. The island city founded by Williams and his friends had proven the wisdom of the pioneer entrepreneurs and had become a center of commerce.

NOTES

CHAPTER 1

1. Samuel May Williams to Sarah Williams, July 23, 1838, Samuel May Williams Papers, Rosenberg Library, Galveston (hereafter cited as Williams Papers).

2. Charles W. Hayes, *Galveston: History of the Island and the City* (Austin: Jenkins Garrett, 1974), 823–830.

3. G. Dorsey to S. M. Williams, Apr. 4, May 9, 1848, Williams Papers; Mirabeau Buonaparte Lamar, *The Papers of Mirabeau Buonaparte Lamar*, eds. Charles Adams Gulick et al. (6 vols.; Austin: A. C. Baldwin, 1921–1927), V, 351; Mary Austin Holley, "Interview with Prominent Texans of Early Days," Mary Austin Holley Papers, Eugene C. Barker Texas History Center, University of Texas at Austin; hereafter cited as BTHC; S. F. Austin to Josiah H. Bell, Aug. 6, 1823, in *The Austin Papers*, ed. Eugene C. Barker (3 vols.; Washington, D.C.: U.S. Government Printing Office, 1924–1928), I, 681–683.

4. Margaret S. Henson, *Samuel May Williams: Early Texas Entrepreneur* (College Station: Texas A & M University Press, 1976), 12, 18, 20; Eugene C. Barker, *The Life of Stephen F. Austin, Founder of Texas, 1793–1836: A Chapter in the Westward Movement of the Anglo-American People* (Austin: University of Texas Press, 1969), 107.

5. Henson, *Samuel May Williams*, 50; Hayes, *Galveston*, 816–819.

6. Henson, *Samuel May Williams*, 63–73.

7. Ibid., 86; genealogical information in possession of the author.

8. Henson, *Samuel May Williams*, 84–85.

9. T. F. McKinney, affidavit applying for relief, c1872, Benjamin C. Franklin Papers, BTHC; Report to the President of the Senate and the Speaker of the House of the State of Texas, January 24, 1848, copy in the Gail Borden, Jr., Collection (Texas History Library of the Daughters of the Republic of Texas, San Antonio). A scaled-down payment was made to both men during the 1850s from funds secured through the Compromise of 1850, but neither was fully recompensed during his lifetime. As late as 1928 the legislature approved a relief bill for some distant McKinney heirs, but there was no funding to make a payment.

10. Memorandum of Seguin Title, Jan. 1833, Galveston City Company Papers (Rosenberg Library, Galveston); T. F. McKinney to S. M. Williams, Mar. 23, 1834,

Michel B. Menard to S. M. Williams, Oct. 9, 1834 (quotation), Williams Papers.

11. Hayes, *Galveston*, 177, 179; Act of the Republic of Texas (Dec. 9, 1836), H. P. N. Gammel (comp.), *The Laws of Texas, 1822–1897* . . . (10 vols.; Austin: Gammel Book Co., 1898), I, 1,328.

12. *Documents Shewing the Manner in Which the Title to the Town Site, on Galveston Island Is Vested in the Trustees* (n. p.: Bailie and Gallaher, 1837), 1–14; Henson, *Samuel May Williams*, 94–96; Hayes, *Galveston*, 260–261. See also the Galveston City Company Papers, Rosenberg Library, Galveston.

13. See Amasa Turner's not totally accurate reminiscence of the hurricane in Hayes, *Galveston*, 277–279; T. F. McKinney to S. M. Williams, July 16, 1837, Oct. 22, 1838, Dec. 10, 1839, Williams Papers.

CHAPTER 2

1. Henson, *Samuel May Williams*, 102–103, 105. The *San Jacinto* was previously known as the *Viper*.

2. T. F. McKinney to S. M. Williams, July 16, 1838, Dec. 10, 1839, Sarah Williams to S. M. Williams, August 20, 1838, Dec. 13, 1838, Dec. 14, 1839, Williams Papers. According to Philip C. Tucker, the houses are identical. Philip C. Tucker to Galveston *Daily News*, June 9, 1935.

3. Galveston County Deed Record, E, 20, A, 570, in Galveston County Clerk's Office, Galveston. For the race track see Francis Cynric Sheridan, *Galveston Island or, A Few Months Off the Coast of Texas: The Journal of Francis C. Sheridan*, ed. Willis W. Pratt (Austin: University of Texas Press, 1954), 49.

4. Nicholas D. Labadie to Anthony LaGrave, Oct. 6, 1838 (1st quotation), Nicholas DeComps Labadie Papers, Rosenberg Library, Galveston; Ashbel Smith, *Yellow Fever in Galveston, Republic of Texas, 1839: An Account of the Great Epidemic* (Austin: University of Texas Press, 1951), 42 (2nd quotation). See also Lucy P. Shaw to Mrs. Jane N. Weston, Dec. 3, 1839 (typescript; Lucy P. Shaw Letters, Rosenberg Library, Galveston).

5. T. F. McKinney to S. M. Williams, Dec. 10, 1839 (quotation), Williams Papers; Lucy P. Shaw to Mrs. Jane N. Weston, Dec. 11, 1838, Feb. 24, Apr. 21, Sept. 9, Oct. 6, 1839, Lucy P. Shaw Letters. The McKinney and Williams ledger for November 1839 to December 1840 (actually a daybook) shows lumber charged to Williams's account on December 21, 1839 (p. 97) by J. C. Shaw, a newcomer from Maine (this ledger is found in the Williams Papers); Building Conservation Technology (Nashville, Tenn.), *Report on the Samuel May Williams House, 1980*, in possession of Galveston Historical Foundation, Galveston (hereafter cited as BCT Report).

6. Subsequent architectural statements are based on the BCT Report unless otherwise noted. Howard Barnstone, *The Galveston That Was* (New York: Macmillan, 1966), 24 (quotation).

7. Mary Austin Holley to Harriet Brand, Nov. 12, 1840 (quotations), Mary Austin Holley Papers, BTHC.

8. Mary Jane (Clemens) Riddle Menard to James Clemens, Jr., Oct. 30, 1844, Mary Clemens Collection, St. Louis University Library (copy in Michel B. Menard File, Historic American Buildings Survey Records, Rosenberg Library, Galveston, hereafter cited as HABSR).

9. BCT Report, 8.

10. Details about the furniture were gleaned from statements and receipts in the Williams Papers and from the inventory of the Williams estate. Patrick H. Butler III, "The Samuel May Williams House of Galveston: A Furnishing Plan," for the Galveston Historical Foundation (Mar. 1, 1980).

11. Genealogical material in the possession of the author; S. M. Williams to Sarah Williams, May 24, 1842, May 19, June 19, 1844, June 23, 1854, Williams Papers.

12. Joseph V. Williams to mother, Aug. 6, 1838, statements to Williams for tuition, July 3, 1839, June 2, 4, 12, 1850, Nov. 5, 1852, subscription, May 11, 1839, Williams Papers.

13. Lucy B. Jones to Mrs. W. H. Jack, Feb. 12, 1842, Jack Family Papers, Rosenberg Library, Galveston.

14. Henson, *Samuel May Williams*, 156, 159.

CHAPTER 3

1. Henson, *Samuel May Williams*, 111–112, 115.
2. Ibid., 136–141.
3. Ibid., 141–146, 162–163.
4. Ibid., 133–134.
5. Ibid., 161–162.
6. Ibid., 162–163.
7. *Texas Freemason* (San Antonio), Aug. 1894; Galveston *Daily News*, July 14, 1894.
8. Undated clippings of obituaries and other material, Tucker Family Papers, Rosenberg Library, Galveston.

CHAPTER 4

1. Sheridan, *Galveston Island*, 30–31 (2nd quotation), 95 (1st quotation).
2. Henry G. Taliaferro, comp., *Cartographic Sources in the Rosenberg Library*, eds. Jane A. Kenamore and Uli Haller (College Station: Texas A & M University Press, 1988), 123.
3. An Act to divorce Thomas F. McKinney. . . ., July 18, 1842, Gammel (comp.), *Laws of Texas*, II, 505; *Nancy McKinney v. Thomas F. McKinney*, Sept. 7, 1842, Galveston District Court, B:153, Galveston District Clerk's Office, Galveston; Galveston County Deed Record, A, 570; T. F. McKinney to S. M. Williams, Nov. 11, 1838, T. F. McKinney Papers, BTHC; Lucy B. Jones to Mrs. W. H. Jack, July 27, 1840, Jack Family Papers; Philip Norbourne Barbour, *Journals of the Late Brevet Major Philip Norbourne Barbour. . . .*, ed. Rhoda van Bibber Tanner Doubleday (New York: G. P. Putnam's Sons, 1936), 116, 118; T. F. McKinney to S. M. Williams, Mar. 25, 1842, Williams Papers.
4. Walter Prescott Webb, H. Bailey Carroll, and Eldon Stephen Branda (eds.), *The Handbook of Texas* (3 vols.; Austin: Texas State Historical Association, 1952, 1976), I, 189; Hayes, *Galveston*, 834–839; David G. McComb, *Galveston: A History* (Austin: University of Texas Press, 1986), 71–72.
5. Joe B. Frantz, *Gail Borden: Dairyman to a Nation* (Norman: University of Oklahoma Press, 1951), 201–221.

6. Galveston County Deed Records, A, 251; various documents in the Menard File (HABSR).

7. Virginia Eisenhour, "The Fabulous Enterpriser: Letters of Michel B. Menard" (unpublished manuscript, n. d.; in possession of Mrs. M. E. Eisenhour, Galveston), 2–6.

8. M. B. Menard to Mrs. Angelique Menard, June 26, 1833, Pierre Menard Collection, Illinois State Historical Library, Springfield (translated typescript copy in possesssion of Virginia Eisenhour, Galveston); Sam Houston to Robert A. Irion, July 7, 1838, in *The Writing of Sam Houston, 1813–1863*, eds. Amelia A. Williams and Eugene C. Barker, 8 vols. (Austin: Pemberton Press, 1970), II, 262; T. F. McKinney to S. M. Williams, Aug. 21, 1838, Williams Papers; Nicholas D. Labadie to Anthony LaGrave, Oct. 6, 1838, Labadie Papers.

9. Galveston County Deed Records, B1, 257, C, 263; United States Seventh Census (1850), Galveston County, Texas, 784; obituary, Galveston *Tri-Weekly News*, Sept. 4, 1856; Hayes, *Galveston*, 811–815; Joseph Franklin, Abstract of Title to South East Quarter of Out Lot 37, Galveston City, copy in Menard File (HABSR).

10. Hayes, *Galveston*, 930–933; Galveston County Tax Rolls, 1840–1847 (microfilm in Rosenberg Library, Galveston); United States Seventh Census (1850), 662; McComb, *Galveston*, 87. In the 1890s this house was divided into three parts and moved. Two of the parts still stand, at Avenue O at Thirty-fifth Street and on Thirty-fifth Street toward the beach. The third part burned.

11. Lucy P. Shaw to Mrs. Jane N. Weston, Aug. 23, 1840, Lucy P. Shaw Letters, Rosenberg Library, Galveston; Galveston County Tax Rolls, 1839–1848 (microfilm in Rosenberg Library, Galveston).

12. Hayes, *Galveston*, 839–841. The Loves were in Houston on March 19, 1839, and left for Galveston on June 20. [Millie Richards (Stone) Gray,] *The Diary of Millie Gray, 1832–1840* . . . (Galveston: Rosenberg Library Press, 1967), 124–125; James Love to Albert Sidney Johnston, various letters from 1837 to 1848, Albert Sidney Johnston Papers, Tulane University Library, New Orleans (copies in possession of the author); United States Seventh Census (1850), 390.

13. Mary Austin Holley, *Mary Austin Holley: The Texas Diary, 1835–1838*, ed. J. P. Bryan (Austin: University of Texas Press, 1965), 29.

14. Barbour, *Journals of the Late Brevet Major Philip Norbourne Barbour. . . .*, 111–117, 118 (2nd quotation), 119, 120 (1st quotation), 121 (3rd and 4th quotations), 122–124, 125 (5th quotation), 126–162.

15. S. M. Williams to Sarah Williams, May 24, 1842, Williams Papers.